loving.

Macy Hudgins

BookLeaf Publishing

India | USA | UK

Presentation by *BookLeaf Publishing*

Web: www.bookleafpub.com

E-mail: info@bookleafpub.com

ISBN: 9789363315440

First edition 2024

To my mom,

The one who has been the greatest example of
unconditional love

ACKNOWLEDGEMENT

I have always dreamed of this collection, but I never had the pieces(or the guts) to try and write it. I finally found the courage because I have had the honor of learning from many wise women, and being friends with the same.

Thank you to my mom. This book is dedicated to you for a reason. You so clearly exemplify what it looks like to love and pursue the Lord. You have taught me many things without even speaking, and much more by your words so layered with grace. I would not be who I am without you. Thank you to my dad. You have shown me what it looks like to have a loving father in my life. I am grateful for the way that you help me work out my problems. You always guide me to sources of truth in a world of confusion, and I cannot thank you enough for that.

To Caroline Davidson, thank you for the way you helped me out when I was struggled to author some of these poems. Our late night conversations helped a lot, and it was refreshing to talk about the Lord with you. I miss you a lot and I am so grateful for your input, and your faith.

To my family and friends, your sacrifice does not go unnoticed. I am not always easy to love, but each of you continually choose to see past my failure. Thank you for being so graceful over the years. I strive to return the same to you.

However, none of this would be possible without my Lord and Savior, Jesus Christ. My greatest gratitude goes to Him. He paid the debt I could never zero out. I am so grateful to be loved by Him. I hope this book helps people understand just how wonderful He is, because He is so worth it.

The Perfect Metaphor

I think fire is the
Perfect
Metaphor for Love.

Sometimes it fizzles
And pops, announcing itself
Loudly, as though it is the
Fourth of July.
But fireworks do not
Stick around,
And just the same
Does love sometimes
Burn out.

It has been a forest fire,
Raging and roiling with
Passion that quakes the
Ground as flaming
Trees are cut down by
Its heat, which only the strongest
Are capable of weathering.
This love is hard to tame,
For it burns so bright
On its own.
And yet, for all the ashes

It gives, Passion tills the
Ground for the
Seeds of tomorrow,
Ridding the soil of rock
And weed so that
Life can find a home
In the earth.

Have you ever lit a
Candle in a dark room?
Love can be this, too,
For sometimes, it is all
That a soul possesses.
Love has been a small light,
But it is no less luminous
Than a forest fire.
It shines brighter still
Because its neighbors are
Pain and Darkness.

Fire warms my hands on
A cold night. In its grasp,
My eyes find themselves
Full of light. It browns my
Marshmallow while I
Watch the summer stars
Shine bright.
Fire fuels my train, and
Cauterizes my wounds;

It cooks my food, and it
Protects me from becoming
Prey to things I cannot fight
In the dark.

The smell of it is on my hair,
Filling up every room in the
Mansion of my soul.

I smell of Love, because I choose
To fan the flame He has
Offered me in exchange for
Wet wood and a pile of ashes.
This is a smoke that does not
Cause my throat to fail.
Rather I breathe the fire
That now burns inside me.

A Book Review

As someone who has
Never been in love,
I do not recommend
Reading Pride and Prejudice.

While the book is
A wonderful read,
It has side effects,
Just like every
Medication
They advertise on TV.

My daydreams are no
Longer full of what ifs,
Rather, they overflow with
Whens.

Jane Austen has turned
Me into a romantic who
Writes poems about
The love she longs for
And plans dates before
There is ever someone
To take me on them.

What am I to do
With all these feelings?
These restless stirrings?

I simply obey them,
For they drive me
Into the arms of a
Bridegroom King who has
Loved me better than
Any man ever could.

I guess I was just too full
Of pride to see Him.

As someone who is beginning
To understand what falling
In love feels like,
I recommend you read
Pride and Prejudice.

Quilting

If you were to ask
Me about love,
I would tell you it is
Costly.
Love has made me a
Patchwork of scars,
Because I trusted in the
Wrong affection to
Stitch me into a
Tapestry of stars.

Sometimes I think of
The threads of tragedy
Woven into me
And I wonder at the way
I was able to stand under
The suffering,
Held together by my
Stitches of scar tissue.

But Love has a way of
Unraveling things.
He stands over me,
With sharp scissors in His
Careful hand,

Taking the blade that cut me
And making my soul smooth
Again.
He slowly works backwards,
Because stitches
Never come out easier
Than they go in.
Piece by piece,
Snip by snip,
He removes what
Causes me to fray.

Love takes the pieces
Of me I never thought
Could be usable,
Let alone beautiful,
And knits them together
Into a mosaic of pain,
Held together by a single
Thread the color of Blood.

Inside Out

Love does not force
Me to color inside the lines.
Rather it gradually
Refines my hand
So that my chaos
Becomes quietly organized.

I am not chastised
For drawing as a
Toddler would,
But told my erratic expression
Is a masterpiece
Unworthy of further
Repression.

Love has a way of showing
Me how to use a coloring book.
Red goes here, yellow there,
Purple goes up, blue goes down,
And green only appears
When there is cranberry sauce around.

Instead of taking away my crayons,
Love introduces me to the
World of coloring-by-number.

Every emotion has a space,
Turning everything I have
Been told about feelings
Inside out.

The Earth In Me

My soul has been a
Piece of rugged rock,
Sharp to the touch,
And unapologetically so.
But over time, a Man
Has loved my points
And my edges enough
To wear them down to
A surface that is merely
Rough.
With His affection,
He has sanded my
Sandpaper soul to a stone
So smooth that
There is no catch
If you run your
Hand across the surface.

I have thrown such stones at Him.

With His kindness, He has
Turned my stone to flesh
That is full of blood and
Full of feeling,
And He has taught me how
I am to love Him.

I always longed for His
Touch, but I never knew
He even desired to be
Loved until my heart
Was capable of such
A sacrifice.

From mountain to ore,
To gritty sea shore,
To pleasing,
To perfect
Though I am still broken,
He has loved the earth
Out of me,
And given me instead
A heart that pursues
Eternity.

Pitbulls and Roses

Love is like a pitbull,
A breed hindered in
Ownership by feelings of
Fear based on one or
Two bad reviews.
Most of the time,
Such feelings find their
Start with the owner.
The pitbull is still just
A dog, still getting excited
About a doggie biscuit,
Yet, it maintains the
Ferocity to defend a
House against intrusion.

So, too, has Love been
Cast in a wrong light
Because so many profess
Pure adoration, only to
Follow it with
The opposite action.
Our shortcomings have
Taught our peers that Love
Is a pitbull, best suited
To be muzzled and chained.

This event has already happened once.

He is not a big man upstairs,
Waiting for a moment to
Smash you under the thumb
Of His judgement.
He is the Bridegroom King,
Waiting at the altar for His
bride(you), hoping to share
His kingdom with her.
He still waits, even though
She may never come to
Recite her vows.

I must ask you this:
Would you go to the owner
Of an overly aggressive pitbulls
For an honest
Explanation of the dog's behavior?

In the same way,
Why go to someone who has
Failed at being a bride to
Learn about the husband?
Why take advice about love
From anywhere except the
Epitome of Love, for He loves
Truth, Himself?

A Table for Two

In a society structured
Around struggling in silence,
My Love does not scurry past
My stumbling spirit.
He sets the table for two,
A dinner date for a bride and Groom;
Intimacy plays a piano in the
Background as we sit together
To talk about my pain.

My mouth opens and the sorrow
That emptied my soul spills
From my stomach.
I am talking around spoonful
Of self-control stew,
A broth of ingredients
Rich in flavor, but numbered few.
When did my hands become holy
Enough to hold the King's cutlery?
I have become
Full on the only feast I was
Ever meant to consume.
My entire life, such a meal has
Been waiting for me,
But a belly full of

Bitter brokenness does
Make room for an much
Of an appetite.

I never thought I would be
A candidate for a romance
Such as this, because at my
Core I am simply unlovable.
I drift to lover after lover,
For my heart is quick to
Forget the wedding band
On my finger.
Yet, Love is so
Indescribably magnificent,
It is no surprise that it
Does not make sense.

The Father's Hand

The day I fell in love with
God was the day I realized
He was in love with me.
He did not contain His
Love to a vase of roses,
Instead giving fields of wildflowers.
He does not love me to
The moon and back,
But made the moon and
Its host, that my eyes might
Overflow with wonder.

The fullness of creation is
The play set He has built for me
In the backyard of this fragmented
Heaven.
He paints the sky afresh every
Morning and night, the sunrise and
Setting all purposed for steering my
Heart towards Him.

I turn my gaze to the expanse
Above and see the stars He
Stitched together in a
Constellation of affection,

The strings of cotton
Knitted together by a
Fathers hand.

Like a Dad, He builds for me.
He constructs a future of good
And prosperous things, and though
He knows best, He gives me a choice.
He loves the smile on my face
As I open the presents He gives
Me just because.

He sits at my side as
I struggle over the homework
Life hands me, patiently
Whispering direction in my ear.
Some things are too
Simple to understand,
And He understands that.
He prepares a feast for me
Each day, but is not angry
When I decide eating it
Is a waste of time; He still cooks.

I was made for
Loving Him, and He made
Me for His Love.
In everything I see, there
Is evidence of the touch

Of my Father. Kindness is not
The story of many, but it is
The story that God writes for
All.
It is time to put the pen back in
The Father's hand.

Grounded

Love holds me close
As I pound my fists
Upon His scarred chest,
A fit of rage flowing from
My impatience.

My mouth, the same that
Has offered many kisses,
Now forms the accusatory
Syllables of "Why?"
I am stranded in a place
I never planned on stopping in,
My flight diverted and delayed.
Gravity has glued me to the gritty ground,
Shackling my perfect agenda into uncertainty.

How frustrating.

My assigned seat feels
Less comfortable by the minute,
And my mind races with all
I might be missing,
But the Pilot receives order from
Air Traffic Control,
And there is weather over

My destination He knows
I cannot weather.
He would rather have me
Disappointed than have me
Dead.

In this House, being
Grounded is not punishing,
It is protecting, proving that
Love cares enough to
Clear the way for my calling.
So I will bear a little while more,
For history tells me that the Pilot
Knows exactly when we'll soar.

Scoreless

Love is not a game,
But the world has
Turned it into one.

"Love" is determined
By what you can do,
And it always seems like
I owe somebody something.
Am I the only person
Who cannot see the scoreboard?
How much you give away
Proclaims what kind of
Person you are.
I just do not remember
When actions became identity,
Instead of what flows from it.

Have we forgotten Love?

He offers Himself
For me, a bride who has
Adulterous tendencies
Branded into her skin,
Enslaving her to sorrow.

Love overlooks my flaws,
But does not ignore them.
I am given over to
Being a cloud.
Still, Love chooses to
Address me by my
Clothing of silver;
He just waits until I am
In a place to address
Where I fall short.
He knows that what I have
To offer is not enough,
So He expects my dependence
To be the telltale of my love.

Yet He does not hold my
Permanent insufficiency
Over my head. He counts instead
The immeasurable amount of
Grace He has sat to the side
For me.

Then all the things that
Keep me cumulonimbus-ly
Puffed up come flowing out.
Love must have alighted on
My walls of silver long
Enough to install floodgates.

Love is not a game
Because it does not keep
A score.
Wasted affection becomes
A source of animosity,
And in Love, there is no
Room for such feeling to stay.
Love is selflessly scoreless,
And He will remain that way.

Man and the Moon

Love is like the moon,
Not always visible,
But always there.
Present even on the
Darkest of nights and the
Brightest of days.

But like the earth,
We sometimes turn our
Back to its gaze,
The same way we turned
Our face away on calvary.
He did not save Himself,
But continued to suffer
So that He might save us;
In all our unfaithfulness,
He chose us all the same.

Just as the moon hangs
In the sky, so too, does
The Son rest over us,
Waiting with Love
In His starry eyes.

We just have to lift
Our eyes
To the sky and
Search for His.

Reflection of Royalty

The more I think
About the complexity
Of love, the more I
Understand that
EVERYTHING
I do stems from
Who and what I
Give my affection.

Growing up, people
Tell us that we are what
We eat, but I have not
Turned into a sandwich.
However, you do indeed
Become what you adore.

Falling in love with the
Wrong things has turned me
Into a monster before, and
That deal is still there.
But I have found a Love
That is greater than monstrosity.
Rather than becoming a mirror
For someone that will pass away,
He invites me to be a reflection

Of royalty, reminding me that
Such a status is in my blood.

Opening a Door

The Big, Bad Wolf failed
To blow down my house
Of hard, red brick,
But Love comes to knock on
My door, being the gentleman
That He is, hoping I will open
It to let Him in.

Knuckles on wood wake
Me from my feverish slumber,
And I come to the door
Dressed in my despair.
My robes, flowy and blue,
Are expansive enough
To swallow me whole.
Sometimes, that feels
Awfully close.
Many times have I stumbled
Over the sorrow I shuttle around,
Leaving my heart riddled with
Bruises that tell of each fall.

Love does not huff and puff
My hurting heart full of the
False promises that have led

To its current state, though
I buy them up like
They are to expire soon.
He utters nothing more than
A question, searching for my
Permission to enter into
The four walls that have
Become my definition of
Protection.

Plain to see, it appears a
Wonderful estate to live in,
But hidden in the shadows
That find vacancy inside is
The hard truth.

I am alone.

But Love is not afraid
Of my habitual isolation.
My hesitance does not
Hinder His quiet consolations.
So we sit on a couch, covered
In clutter and confusion, and
We just sit.

Somehow His silence is
Saying everything all at once.
He is Patient, and He does not pry,

Even though He already knows why,
He waits to be told the reason I cry.
He is Kind, a hand on my shoulder,
Finally a touch I do not shudder
At, because He does not play controller.
He is Humble, spending His time with
The brokenhearted who love to sift
The ashes of joy turned bereft.

He does not look at my mess
With disgust, and I digest the
Thought that He might just have
Come to help me out of
The pit I dig for myself with
My own two hands.
When I build enough courage
To look into His brown oceans
That push and pull with
His love for me, I do not
See what I thought I
Would always have seen.
There is no judgement in the
Tears that pour from His sea.
He does not turn His face from me.
He is not afraid of what He has
Already seen.

And just like that,
My house begins to crumble,

My muffled heart begins to
Mumble of pain and sorrow
Stuck in a storehouse
Guarded by the fears of
Tomorrow.
What was a trickle turns
To a stream,
And what was blue
Becomes green. The stream
Turns to a raging river,
Green tinged with yellow
Begins to deliver.
And suddenly, the water
Quits its racing,
And my heart
Unlearns its bracing.
I stand motionless in
The bright yellow of the
Son, and it warms skin
I thought would never
Be warm ever again.

And it took no words at all,
Just an opening of a door
For this house to become a home
Once more.

Just Too Heavy

Sometimes, Love is
Most apparent when
I have lost it all.
It is when I make my
Bed in the ashes of my
Dreams that His presence
Is most felt next to me.
He whispers His affections
In the depths of my sorrow,
Reminding this forgetful soul
That it is not the sole sufferer here.

Love takes the brunt
Of my despair and holds
The burden of my joy,
For He bears all things.
There is none so capable
Of standing under the
Weight of my mistakes
In order to carry what
I myself crumple under
Time and again.

He allowed my splintered
Soul to dig into His

Shoulder, occupied by ridges
And wounds, somehow
Sharp enough to sand me down.
All He asks for in return is
Everything;
It is not much.
But it is hard, sometimes,
To give everything in a land
Championed by privilege.
So, He graciously helps me
By taking it away.

I have learned that Love
Takes, too.
If love is true, it
Does not let the
Object of its affection
Continue to push around
An IV cart dripping poison.

Love, too, involves losing
Things, letting go, of what
We call precious.
He was so willing to die
For me,
Because some crosses
Are just too heavy
For humans to carry.

Dead Man's Friend

In a land of dry bones,
Love visited a friend,
Coming to his bed,
Weeping, even though

He knew the Author

Had not yet put away
His pen.

He did not bring a
Bundle of flowers,
So His hands were
Ready to hold those
Of another, embracing a
Grieving sister, and mother.

The gift He gave Lazarus
Is the same one I now possess,
Only I did not have a headstone,
I just made my home in a tomb.
But Love called me out of
The inheritance left by Eve,
To stand at His side
As royalty.

Why would a holy man would bend
His knee to the mire for
Me, to help me out of it,
To see me free?
There is no friend like the
Man Named Jesus,
The guy who wore my
Grave clothes for me.

He knows the Author
Has still not put away
His pen.

If Not For Love

Because I have loved
I have lost so much,
For the Subject of my
Affection bids me to change
In all the ways I never could,
If not for Love.

And yet, He is patient
As He waits for me to walk
With more Patience.
He is kind, unafraid to
Remind me that even trees
Struggle to hold onto
Their leaves sometimes.

He does not care that I fail,
Just that I try,
For He is no stranger to
The difficulty of change.
He is gracious as He reaches
Down to pick me up
After yet another flailing fall.

He does not seek my perfection,
Rather, His eyes search for a
Heart full of devotion.

If not for Love,
I do not think I would be capable of
Such a postured heart.
But He is loving, I am learning,
While He waits for my center
To surrender to His hand.

Red Ink

I had written myself out
Of the story already
Scripted for me.
I could not play the
Part of holy, so the only
Place fit for me was the
"Did Not Finish" pile of
Paper next to be burned to ash.

But I was writing with
Ink made invisible by Blood.
Lemon juice nor heat cannot
Reveal the tale I spun
In the midst of my misery.
It has been erased from
The textbooks
Of history.

Someone greater than I
Has rewritten my
Biography to contain
The glory He planned
For me long ago, but
My fallacies and failings
Foreclosed on my ability

To handle the yoke
That comes with it.

He took the light
That I shattered
And scattered,
And gathered me up,
Piece by piece,
And wove me together
In a constellation of red ink.
My biography is not a
Story of my life anymore,
For my life is hidden
In the perfect one He
Wrote for me.

Teachers make corrections
With their red scratching,
But He makes perfection.

Places, Everyone

The more I think
About the complexity
Of love, the more I
Understand that
EVERYTHING
I do stems from
Who and what I
Give my affection.

Growing up, people
Tell us that we are what
We eat, but I have not
Turned into a sandwich.
However, you do indeed
Become what you adore.

Falling in love with the
Wrong things has turned me
Into a monster before, and
That deal is still there.
But I have found a Love
That is greater than monstrosity.
Rather than becoming a mirror
For someone that will pass away,
He invites me to be a reflection

Of royalty, reminding me that
Such a status is in my blood.